SPOTLIGHT ON NATURE
KANGAROO

PAMELA DELL

CREATIVE EDUCATION · CREATIVE PAPERBACKS

Published by Creative Education and Creative Paperbacks
P.O. Box 227, Mankato, Minnesota 56002
Creative Education and Creative Paperbacks are imprints
of The Creative Company
www.thecreativecompany.us

Design and production by Blue Design, Inc.
Art direction by Tom Morgan

Images by Alamy Stock Photo/Arco / TUNS, 21; Dreamstime/Anankkml, 1, Jan Pokorný, 9, Ken Griffiths, 16, Martin Pelanek, 14; flickr/Biodiversity Heritage Library, 8, 10, 14, 16, 20, 22; Getty Images/Jami Tarris, 6, 23, Jan Abadschieff, 15, Joao Inacio, 10, John Carnemolla/Australian Picture Library, 24, John White Photos, 27, Lea Scaddan, 11, Matt Deakin, 12; Pexels/Ethan Brooke, 17, Sergey Guk, 28, Valeriia Miller, 28; Shutterstock/Andrey_Fokin, 4–5, Svietlieisha Olena, cover; Unsplash/Seiji Seiji, 26; Wikimedia Commons/Charles J. Sharp, 29, Dmitry Makeev, 3, 6, 29, Howard Cheng, 29, PotMart186, 18

Every effort has been made to contact copyright holders for material reproduced in this book. Any omissions will be rectified in subsequent printings if notice is given to the publisher.

Copyright © 2026 Creative Education, Creative Paperbacks
International copyright reserved in all countries. No part of this book may be reproduced in any form without written permission from the publisher.

Library of Congress Cataloging-in-Publication Data
Names: Dell, Pamela author
Title: Kangaroo / by: Pamela Dell.
Description: Mankato, Minnesota : Creative Education and Creative Paperbacks, [2026] | Series: Spotlight on nature | Includes bibliographical references and index. | Audience: Ages 10-13 | Audience: Grades 4-6 | Summary: "An immersive wildlife book for upper-elementary and middle-school readers, featuring a captivating kangaroo family narrative, stunning photography, and educational tools like infographics, a glossary, and an index. Explores species, habitats, and conservation, making it perfect for nature lovers and young conservationists"— Provided by publisher.
Identifiers: LCCN 2025017540 (print) | LCCN 2025017541 (ebook) | ISBN 9798895810774 library binding | ISBN 9798896800309 paperback | ISBN 9798895812037 ebook
Subjects: LCSH: Kangaroos—Juvenile literature
Classification: LCC QL737.M35 D454 2026 (print) | LCC QL737.M35 (ebook) |DDC 599.35/987—dc23/eng/20250711
LC record available at https://lccn.loc.gov/2025017540
LC ebook record available at https://lccn.loc.gov/2025017541

Printed in the United States

CONTENTS

MEET THE FAMILY   4
Red Kangaroos of Australia

LIFE BEGINS   7
FEATURED FAMILY
Welcome to the World   8
First Meal   10

EARLY ADVENTURES   13
FEATURED FAMILY
Trial Runs   14
Give It a Try   16

LIFE LESSONS   19
FEATURED FAMILY
This Is How It's Done   20
Practice Makes Perfect   22

A TWO-SIDED STORY   25

Family Album Snapshots   28
Words to Know   30
Learn More   31
Index   32

MEET THE FAMILY

RED KANGAROOS
of Australia

Australia is a land of great diversity. Much of it has a hot desert climate. But there are also wetlands, plains, and forests. Among the country's 24,000 native plant **species** are eucalyptus and tea trees, and numerous wildflowers. The emu and the dangerous cassowary are only two of Australia's 597 bird species. The country is also home to koalas, wombats, and many other animal species, but no creature embodies the spirit of the nation quite like the kangaroo.

Kangaroos are highly social animals, living in groups known as mobs that typically consist of 10 or more individuals. After a short gestation period of about 33 days, a female prepares for the arrival of her **joey** by carefully cleaning the pouch on her belly, which will serve as her baby's home for the coming months. When the tiny, underdeveloped joey is born, it instinctively makes its way into the pouch, where it will continue to grow until it is strong enough to venture out on its own.

CLOSE-UP
Pouch

A female marsupial's pouch, or *marsupium*, is a hairless, expandable pocket lined with sweat glands and strong, stretchy muscles. She can tighten the muscles to keep her joey in or out.

CHAPTER ONE
LIFE BEGINS

Australia is both a southern hemisphere nation and an entire continent. It is called the land "down under" because it lies farther south than almost every other country. Australia remained isolated from the rest of the world for millions of years. This has given it a wide range of unique and unusual animal species. One of these is the kangaroo, a **marsupial**. The four main kangaroo species live only in Australia. As herbivores, they eat grasses, flowers, fruit, leaves, and mosses. Their few predators are wild Australian dogs called dingoes as well as humans and some **raptors**.

Kangaroos range widely in size. Although males are much bigger, females are faster. Depending on species, these animals weigh between 40 and 200 pounds (18 to 91 kilograms). Standing, they measure anywhere from 3 to 8 feet (0.9 to 2.4 meters) tall.

Red kangaroos, found throughout most of Australia, are the world's largest marsupial. They are also Australia's largest land mammal. Male red

KANGAROO MILESTONES

2 MONTHS
- Eyes open

4 MONTHS
- Is able to hop

kangaroos have orange-red fur. Females are usually bluish-gray. Both have black-and-white cheek patches and ear-to-mouth white stripes.

The second-largest species is the eastern grey, sometimes called the great grey. This species lives in forests and scrubby vegetation in eastern Australia. They are light gray in color with a darker face and a tail ending in a dark tip.

The western grey lives in woodlands throughout southern Australia west of the Great Dividing Range. They look similar to eastern greys, but western greys' faces are broader and dark brown, with white-edged ears and a pale throat.

The antilopine kangaroo belongs to the marsupial family, which also includes wallabies and wallaroos. Sometimes called the antilopine wallaby,

CLOSE-UP
Hind Feet

Kangaroos have enormous feet, handy for launching into long, powerful leaps forward. Kangaroo legs aren't made for walking. Their hind feet move together. When a predator comes lurking, kangaroos will pound the ground with their feet to warn other kangaroos.

—— FEATURED FAMILY ——

Welcome to the World

A mother red kangaroo licks a vertical strip of fur up her belly. Her baby has just been born, no bigger than a grape. He's blind and weighs less than 1 ounce (2 grams). The joey has a lot of work to do now. Using his tiny forearms, he claws his way up that strip of damp fur. It is his pathway into his mother's hairless pouch. He crawls inside. He is safe now, his skin warmed by hers. All his mother has to do is occasionally clean the pouch.

it inhabits northern Australia's grasslands, tropical savannas, and dry, rocky regions. Antilopines range in color from grayish-brown to reddish-brown with thick, short fur.

Male kangaroos are not family-oriented. Raising a joey is all up to the female. But mother kangaroos have little work to do when it comes to an infant joey. They don't even handle their babies. Once inside the pouch, the joey grows gradually and steadily. It will be a while before the joey gets even a glimpse of the wide world outside.

(5) **MONTHS**

▸ Begins peeking out of the pouch

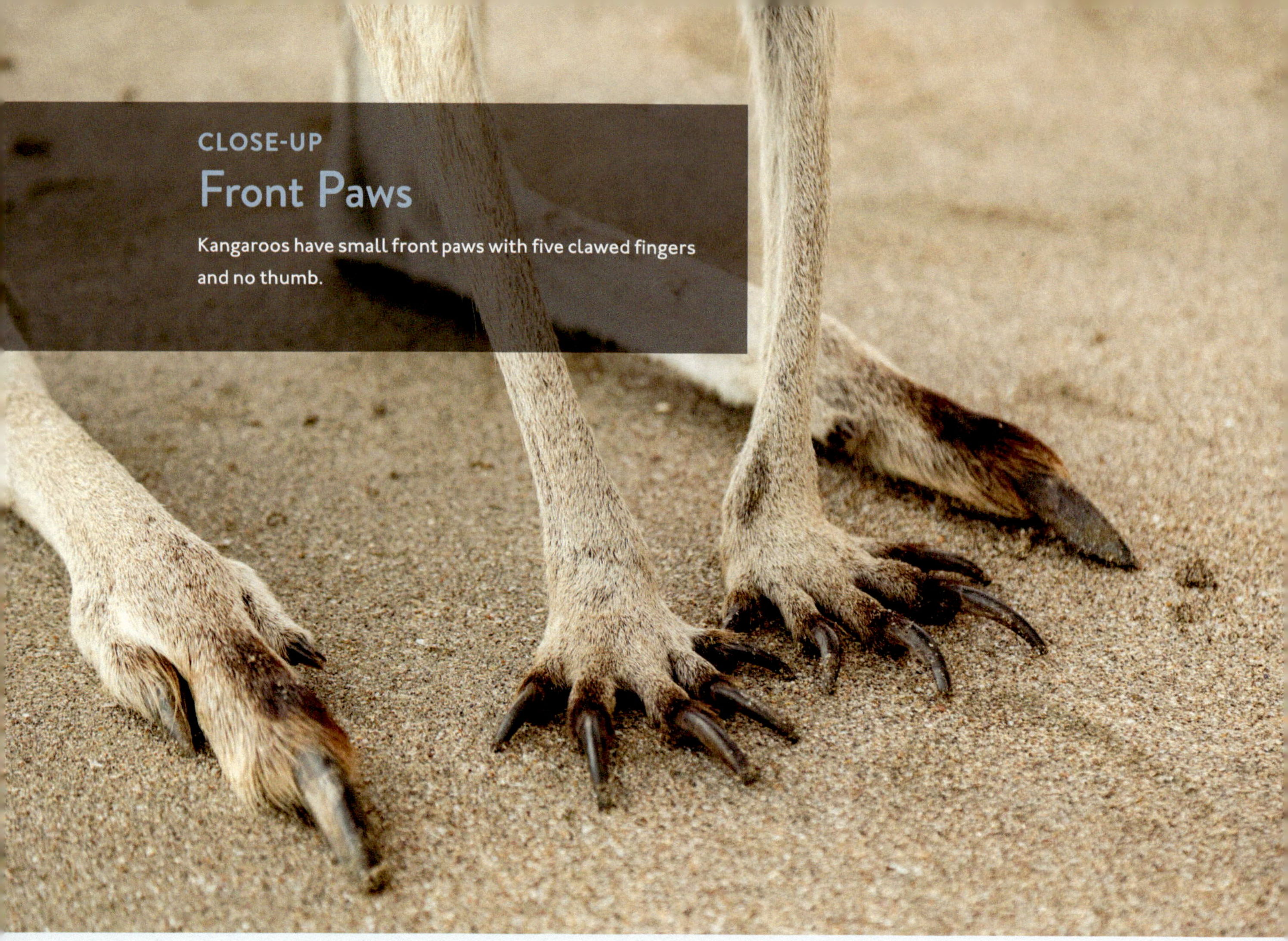

CLOSE-UP
Front Paws

Kangaroos have small front paws with five clawed fingers and no thumb.

— FEATURED FAMILY —

First Meal

Once in the pouch, the pink, hairless baby kangaroo latches on to one of his mother's four nipples, or teats. Once this happens, the teat inflates inside the joey's mouth. This keeps him attached to his food source until his jaw develops and he can **suckle** on his own. Deep down in the pouch's warmth, he will feed fulltime on his mother's high protein milk. As he begins to grow, his eyes will open. His fur gradually grows in. He is finally starting to look like a real "roo."

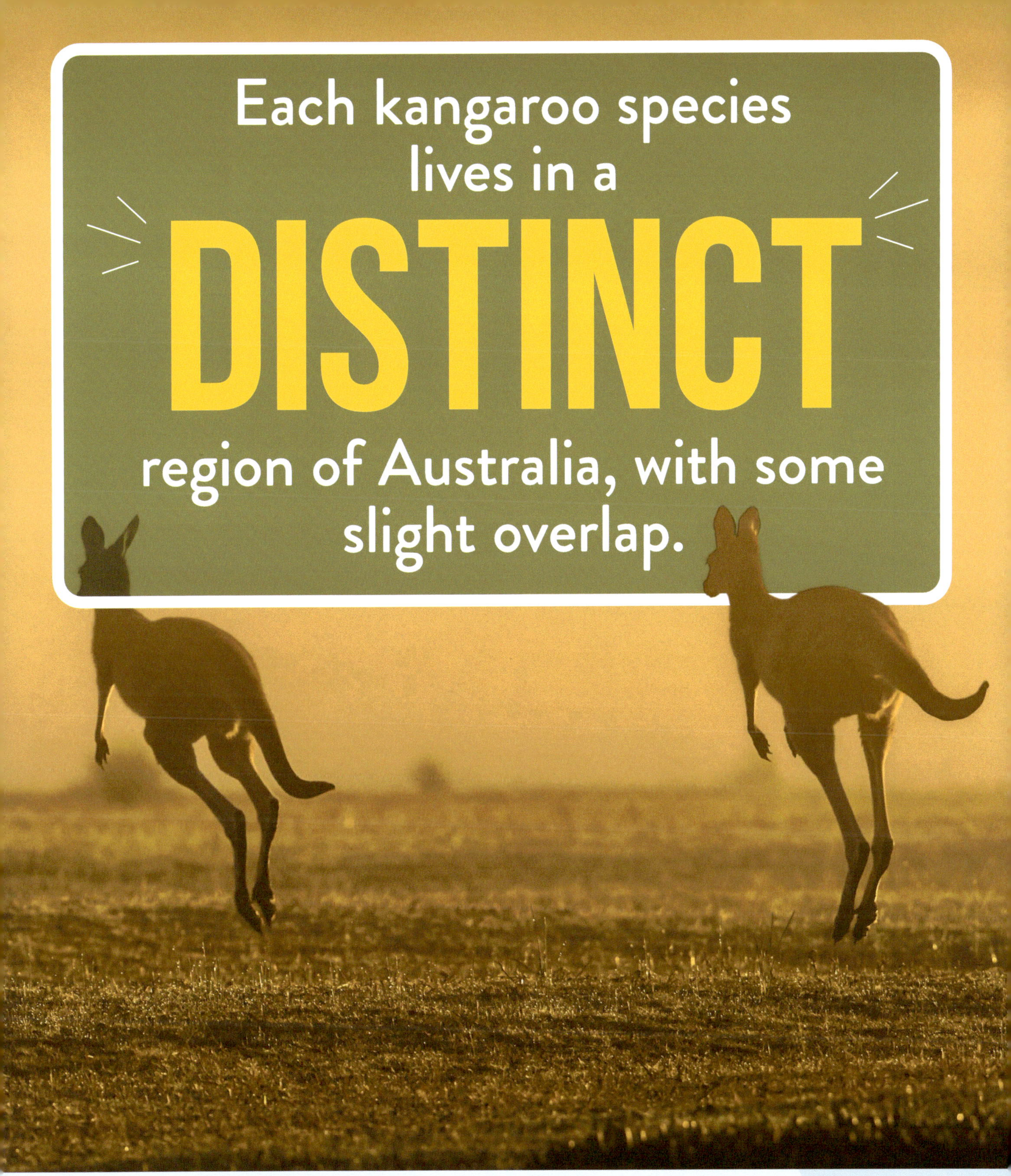

Each kangaroo species lives in a **DISTINCT** region of Australia, with some slight overlap.

⑥ **MONTHS**

▸ Begins leaving the pouch for short periods

LIFE BEGINS 11

CLOSE-UP
Tail

Kangaroo tails are heavily muscled and have nearly as many vertebrae as a human spine. The kangaroo pushes down with its tail to leap forward. The tail provides the most momentum for movement. This is partly why scientists consider the tail a fifth limb.

CHAPTER TWO
EARLY ADVENTURES

Unlike many other animals, most kangaroo species mate at any time of year. The only exception is the eastern grey, which usually mates in spring or early summer. Although they are born hairless and with eyes sealed shut, other parts of a joey's body are well developed at birth—such as the front legs and fingers, nostrils, and tongue. This early development is a plus for survival.

After about five months, little joeys begin peeking out of their private pocket—their mother's pouch. This may vary slightly by species. But the stronger her baby gets, the more eager it is to experience the world. A joey spends many weeks just watching what's going on without actually getting out of the pouch. If its mother is on the run, it's a wild ride for her baby.

At some point, the joey becomes strong enough and brave enough to briefly leave the pouch. The joey exercises its muscles as it learns to stand up and hop. But during their young lives, joeys are very close to their

8-11 MONTHS

- Leaves pouch for good but continues to suckle

CLOSE-UP
Almighty Breath

Kangaroos breathe easily during intense exercise. As they hop, their gut bounces, which automatically inflates and deflates their lungs.

— FEATURED FAMILY —

Trial Runs

At about five months old, the red kangaroo joey first begins peeking out of the pouch. His body is covered in soft fur now. His ears are long and pointed. His mother carries him as she goes about her grazing. He may graze a little too from the pouch. About a month later, the joey is ready to experience the world on his own. He springs out of the pouch—but not for long. He takes many short exploratory trips. Then he dives back in again, safe and sound.

mothers. At this stage, they never stray too far from her. Mother kangaroos teach their joeys how to groom themselves and how and where to **graze**. Joeys also learn to be alert for danger by watching their mothers' signals. If its mother becomes alarmed by some threat, a joey will dive headfirst back into the pouch. Now the little roo is in its safety zone—upside down. But a quick somersault fixes that!

(12) **MONTHS**

- Stops suckling

EARLY ADVENTURES

CLOSE-UP
Teeth

Kangaroo teeth work hard. Their molars wear down and fall out from grinding tough plants, but new ones keep growing in.

— FEATURED FAMILY —

Give It a Try

For a couple months now, the red kangaroo joey has been spending more and more time out of the pouch. He has gradually learned his mother's social behavior and how she schedules her activities. When he is outside the pouch, he interacts more and more with his mother. They groom each other, graze together, and play. He jumps at her, biting at her ears and her tail. When he strays off, he and his mother communicate by sounds. They make soft grunting, clicking, and clucking noises. This new world is fun!

A joey will **GRAZE** from the pouch, sticking head and arms outside it.

(2) YEARS

▸ Kangaroos reach sexual maturity

CLOSE-UP
Embryonic Diapause
If a mother kangaroo gets pregnant while a joey is still in the pouch, she pauses the new baby's growth. until the pouch is empty. This is called **embryonic diapause**.

CHAPTER THREE
LIFE LESSONS

Sooner or later, a young joey must leave the pouch permanently. For red kangaroos, this happens at around eight months of age. Other species get to stay a few months longer. But when the time comes to leave, the joey has no say in the matter. Rather, its mother is the one who decides when the joey gets kicked out for good.

She selects the safest possible time and place to do this. This means a spot with less risk of predators or other dangers. She also avoids the mob. Until now, her joey has stuck close by her side. If she allows the young roo to join the mob too soon, it may attempt to suckle another female and be rejected.

Once the joey is permanently out on its own, the pouch is no longer available for protection. Its mother won't let it back in. Sometimes this is because another baby is on the way. But all is not lost. A joey "at

5 YEARS	6-7 YEARS
▸ Males fully grown	▸ Males reach sexual maturity

foot"—out but remaining with its mother—still needs to suckle. So the mother will allow her young one to stick its head back inside the pouch to eat. If her pouch is inhabited, both joeys will feed on their mother's milk together.

When they have almost reached adulthood, male kangaroos disperse, or leave the mob. They wander widely until they find a new group to join. Many females stay permanently near or within their mother's habitat range.

Depending on species, kangaroos can live anywhere from about eight to 17 years in the wild. But male kangaroos generally have a much shorter lifespan than females. All kangaroos are most likely to die when they've just left the pouch for good or shortly afterward. But males also become

FEATURED FAMILY

This Is How It's Done

The young red kangaroo is nearly eight months old now. His mother is expecting another baby. He is still allowed to put his head into the pouch to suckle, but she will no longer let him climb inside. He doesn't play with his mother anymore either. He has turned his attention to other juvenile males around his own size. The young males practice play-boxing. Their matches help determine how important each of them is in the mob. As adults, they will fight seriously, and sometimes bitterly, for mates.

10 YEARS

▸ End of life for males in the wild

LIFE LESSONS 21

very vulnerable when they leave their home range. Only about five percent of males survive beyond six or seven years. Besides predators, accidents, and diseases, males use up a lot of energy competing against each other for mates. Large adult males, being big and strong, have fewer risks. But any kangaroo that survives leaving the pouch may live many more years.

CLOSE-UP
Boxing Battles

Male kangaroos fight upright, using their tails for balance. They punch, kick, and wrestle by wrapping their arms around each other.

— FEATURED FAMILY —

Practice Makes Perfect

Now nearly full-grown, the young red kangaroo **forages** on his own. His mother has taught him everything he needs to know. Now it is time for him to disperse, or leave his mother's mob. He must find his own territory, and a new mob. One evening at dusk, danger threatens as he drinks from a river. A dingo is on his trail. Before the dog can attack, the kangaroo leaps into the river. A strong swimmer, he soon reaches the other side. He bounds away, ready for his life as an adult.

Males burn lots of ENERGY fighting for mates.

12 YEARS
- End of life for females in the wild

CHAPTER FOUR

A TWO-SIDED STORY

Australia's **coat of arms** shows a kangaroo and an emu, a big native bird. Neither of these animals can move backward, making them fitting symbols of a nation committed to progress. It's no surprise that the kangaroo is one of Australia's most iconic symbols. They are big, unique to Australia, and there are just so many of them.

The kangaroo population is in the tens of millions. It varies from year to year and from one region to another, but there are easily 35 or 40 million total. So all four species are considered of least concern on the **IUCN** endangered species list.

In today's world, with so many animal species at risk of **extinction**, this is a good thing. But there is a dark side to the story. Because wild kangaroos are so numerous, the Australian government allows "sustainable harvesting." This means that anyone with a license can legally hunt kangaroos. Each year the government sets a limit on how many kangaroos can be killed, or harvested. It is typically a low percentage, maybe about 15 percent of the population. And usually this limit is not even met, so that's another positive.

CLOSE-UP
Mother's Milk

Amazingly, mother kangaroos can make different kinds of milk at the same time. Each milk fits the needs of a joey's age, so two nursing joeys may be drinking entirely different types of milk.

So far, the story sounds reasonable. Kangaroos are hunted for their meat and their fur. Their hides are also used for shoes, gloves, and other leather products. The government gives guidelines meant to ensure these killings, or "cullings," are humane. But animal welfare activists around the globe are loudly protesting the sometimes gruesome methods these hunters use. The joeys are especially helpless. If their mothers are killed, they are left to starve and die or are killed themselves.

The activists' outcry has led to at least one major positive change. For years, major athletic shoe companies relied on kangaroo leather, fueling commercial kangaroo hunting. But after discovering the shocking truth about how kangaroos are killed, many of these companies have stopped buying kangaroo leather for their shoes.

No matter what, none of the four main kangaroo species is likely to go extinct. Advocating for more humane practices in commercial kangaroo hunting is a cause worth supporting. No kangaroo should have to suffer at the hands of a human being.

FAMILY ALBUM
SNAPSHOTS

The scientific name for kangaroos, "Macropus," comes from two Greek words. These words are *macros* and *pous*, which together mean "longfoot."

As well as kangaroos, some other marsupials include koalas, opossums, and wallabies.

Male kangaroos are called bucks, boomers, or jacks. Other names for females include does, flyers, and jills.

A mob might consist of one or two large, dominant males, several females and their joeys, plus a few younger males.

The number of kangaroos in a mob can vary. Ten is common. **Antilopine** mobs are sometimes as large as 30 kangaroos.

28

Kangaroos sometimes give birth to twins, but rarely. When they do, one of them usually dies quickly.

Joeys usually take their first trip out of the pouch during the nighttime.

The kangaroo is the only large animal that relies on hopping as its main way to get around.

A kangaroo's normal hopping speed is around 82 feet (25 kilometers) per hour. A single forward bound can take them up to about 30 feet (9 m).

According to research, most **eastern grey** and **red kangaroos** are "left-handed." That is, they mostly use their left paw for tasks like grooming and feeding.

The **antilopine** kangaroo is often most active during the day. Other species are mostly out at dusk and dawn.

WORDS to Know

coat of arms a visual symbol that represents a person, a family, or a nation

embryonic diapause
 a natural pause in an embryo's development, this delay helps time the birth for better survival

extinct no longer in existence

forage search widely for food

graze to feed on lands covered by grasses

IUCN International Union for Conservation of nature, an organization that monitors worldwide animal populations

joey a young kangaroo

marsupial a mammal whose females have a marsupium, or pouch, in which its young grow and develop

raptor eagles, owls, hawks, and other birds of prey that hunt animals for food

species a group of living things that have shared characteristics and are able to reproduce with one another

suckle to feed on milk by sucking on a nipple, or teat

LEARN MORE

Books

Gish, Melissa. *Kangaroos (Living Wild series)*. Minneapolis, MN: The Creative Company, 2024

Gaillard, Isis. *Kangaroos: Photos and Fun Facts for Kids (Kids Learn with Pictures series)*. New York, NY: Infobase, Learn With Facts, 2020.

McDougal, Anna. *The Strange Life Cycle of a Kangaroo*. New York, NY: Rosen Publishing, 2025.

Websites

"Kangaroo facts for kids." Kiddle.

https://kids.kiddle.co/Kangaroo

"Kangaroo." Britannica Kids.

https://kids.britannica.com/kids/article/kangaroo/353331

"Kangaroo Information And Facts For Kids." Active Wild. https://www.activewild.com/kangaroo-information-and-facts-for-kids/

Documentaries

Baveystock, Sacha; Chambers, Dan; Davies, Ashley; Stebbing, Phil [producers]. "Secret Life of the Kangaroo." [documentary series] Streams on Apple TV, Hulu, Pluto TV, 2020.

Clere, Kate McIntyre, McIntyre, Mick. "Kangaroo: A Love-Hate Story." Second Nature Films, 2017.

Dalton, Bettina; Rebecca Vallis [directors]. "The Kangaroo King." Disney+, 2015.

Snook, Sarah [narrator]. "Kangaroo Valley." Netflix, 2022.

Note: Every effort has been made to ensure that any websites listed above were active at the time of publication. However, because of the nature of the Internet, it is impossible to guarantee that these sites will remain active indefinitely or that their contents will not be altered.

Visit

SAN DIEGO ZOO SAFARI PARK
Walk among the park's grey kangaroos in the grasslands of Kangaroo Walk in Walkabout Australia.
2920 Zoo Drive
San Diego, CA 92101

NORTH GEORGIA WILDLIFE & SAFARI PARK
Feed kangaroos and see joeys in the pouch when you sign up for the zoo's "kangaroo experience."
2912 Paradise Valley Rd
Cleveland, GA 30528

NEW ENGLAND'S FRANKLIN PARK ZOO
Spot lots of kangaroos, emus, and other Australian animals on the Outback Trail.
1 Franklin Park Road
Boston, MA 02121

THE KANGAROO SANCTUARY
Celebrate the beautiful red kangaroos on a guided sunset tour down under.
PO Box 4921
Alice Springs, NT, 0871, Australia

INDEX

animal Welfare, 26
Australia, 4, 7, 8, 9, 11, 25
boxing, 20, 22
breathing, 14
communication, 16
development, 13
dispersal, 20, 22
embryonic diapause, 18
grooming, 15, 16, 29
habitat, 9, 20

harvesting, 25
marsupial, 7, 8, 28
mob, 19, 20, 22, 28
pouch, 4, 6, 8, 9, 10, 11, 13, 14, 15, 16, 17, 18, 19, 20, 22, 29
predators, 7, 8, 19, 22
Red Kangaroo, 4, 7, 8, 14, 16, 19, 20, 22, 24
tail, 8, 12, 16, 22
teeth, 16